Young Pathfind

Are you sitting com

Telling stories to young language learners

The Young Pathfinder series

The literacy link (YPF9)
by Catherine Cheater and Anne Farren

Grammar is fun (YPF8)
by Lydia Biriotti

Making the link
Relating languages to other work in the school (YPF7)
by Daniel Tierney and Malcolm Hope

Let's join in!
Rhymes, poems and songs (YPF6)
by Cynthia Martin with Catherine Cheater

First steps to reading and writing (YPF5)
by Christina Skarbek

Keep talking
Teaching in the target language (YPF4)
by Peter Satchwell

Are you sitting comfortably?
Telling stories to young language learners (YPF3)
by Daniel Tierney and Patricia Dobson

Games and fun activities (YPF2)
by Cynthia Martin

Catching them young (YPF1)
by Peter Satchwell and June de Silva

CILT, the National Centre for Languages, seeks to promote a greater national capability in languages. CILT is a registered Charity and provides expertise and support for education, business and the wider community to help develop multilingualism and intercultural competence in all sectors of society.

CILT supports the implementation of the National Languages Strategy and has been managing the Early Language Learning Initiative on behalf of the Department for Education and Skills since 1999.

Young Pathfinder 3

A CILT series for primary language teachers

Are you sitting comfortably?

Telling stories to young language learners

Daniel Tierney and Patricia Dobson

The views expressed in this book are those of the authors and do not necessarily represent the views of CILT.

Acknowledgements

I should like to thank the teachers in the Scottish primary schools involved in language learning whose work on storytelling it has been my privilege to witness. Also Fay Humphreys, the University of Strathclyde, for the illustration on p14 and Loreta Stewart, the University of Strathclyde, for her helpful comments and advice.
DJT

I would like to thank the SOED pilot projects for their work on storytelling during my time as NDO. On many occasions they developed ideas given to them, added their own and shared their successes with others, myself included. Special thanks are due to Margaret Hutcheon for allowing me to use one of her forward plans in this book and to my colleagues, Alison Hurrell and Kate Bannerman, who contributed greatly to the work on storytelling in the pilot projects and who will recognise some of our joint efforts in this book.
PMD

First published 1995
Copyright © 1995 Centre for Information on Language Teaching and Research
ISBN 1 874016 49 6

Cover by Neil Alexander
Printed in Great Britain by Hobbs the Printers Ltd, Totton, Hampshire

Published by the Centre for Information on Language Teaching and Research,
20 Bedfordbury, Covent Garden, London WC2N 4LB.

Contents

Why storytelling?

Any parent or primary teacher will testify to the success of telling stories to children: the story grips the imagination of the child, the child listens carefully, tries to predict what will happen next, offers his or her own contribution and comment to the illustrations that accompany the story, joins in the story when the text is familiar and expresses an opinion at the ending of the story. Such was the potential of storytelling that we knew we were on to a winner with it in the early stages of the pilot projects set up by the Scottish Office Education Department to introduce a foreign language to pupils in primary school. Primary teachers already had an expertise in telling stories to their class and were familiar with appropriate stories for young children: all we had to do was to transfer this success into the foreign language. The success of the work undertaken in many classes in Scotland is clear in that storytelling is popular with both pupils and teachers and is an important element of the foreign language programme in many primary schools in Scotland.

 WHAT DOES LISTENING TO A STORY BRING TO PUPILS?

- In the early stages of learning a foreign language it is easier to listen and understand than to read and understand, particularly when the story is accompanied by gestures and mime and pictures are used to illustrate what is being said.
- Listening to a story in the foreign language contributes to developing listening skills in general as pupils search for 'clues' in the form of familiar words, words which they can recognise in English, content themselves with understanding only some of what they hear and make sensible deductions.
- Telling a story gives pupils a model for pronunciation, particularly if they are encouraged to participate, answer questions and repeat words during the telling of the story.
- Most pupils seem to enjoy listening to stories and are not put off by the foreign language.

FLASHCARDS, OVERHEAD TRANSPARENCIES OR BOOKS?

By and large the choice is yours! Some teachers prefer to use flashcards which depict the basic outline of the story, others prefer overhead transparencies (OHTs), others prefer to use a book, sometimes an English one which they have adapted, sometimes one already written in the foreign language. Frequently the choice will depend on what is available for the story that you want to tell. Inevitably, there are advantages and disadvantages to all three ways.

- Flashcards and OHTs are visually attractive and can stimulate pupil participation during the telling of the story. OHTs can be used to vary the delivery of the story and, along with flashcards, are useful for activities before and after the initial telling of the story, something which is developed further in Chapters 1 and 3. However, time and artistic skills or access to copyright free drawings are required in creating the cards and OHTs if those available commercially are not suitable.

- The advantage of using a book in English is that it will probably be in school already: this is instant preparation! It may be too that pupils are already familiar with the story; this can help them in understanding the foreign language. You can alter the text to get the level of language that is appropriate for your class, you can block out English text or you can put paper over the English text which is only stuck at the top to allow pupils to lift the paper to see the English if they choose to read the story themselves later (perhaps with a cassette to accompany it).

Some teachers have successfully used books already written in the foreign language. This adds an authenticity which appeals to pupils, but you have to be careful when selecting the book. Some can be very difficult, e.g. one version of *Snow White* in German uses a great variety of tenses, language structures and vocabulary that makes it totally unsuitable for use in class. Tenses can be a problem in books written for speakers of that language because of the frequent use of past tense, including the past historic in French. Teachers who have adapted their stories from texts in English have tended to use the present tense after the initial '*Once upon a time there was . . .*'

WHAT TYPE OF STORY WORKS IN THE FOREIGN LANGUAGE?

So many stories have been successful for a variety of reasons. If you, the teacher, like the story and tell it in a way that suits your class, both in terms of the foreign language skills of the pupils and by choosing a story which will appeal to their interests, you are well on the way to success. There are, however, some guidelines about the type of story that has worked well for many teachers:

- Traditional tales or familiar stories have worked because pupils know what happens in the story and can use this prior knowledge to deal with more complex language.
Fewer activities to make the pupils familiar with the language of the story are needed because they know the story already. However, this does not detract from their enjoyment in listening to the story again: somehow or other, it seems different in the foreign language, quite simply because of the challenge involved in trying to understand what is being said.

- A story that has a definite link to a language area being covered, e.g. animals and *Dear zoo*, allows for further practice on a specific language area, calling on previous knowledge and extending it through the story.

- A story that you have created yourself to practise certain points of language or to deal with a certain theme, e.g. *Simon is ill* (see Chapter 5), or have adapted from a well-known story means that it is tailored to suit a particular class, and can be easily adapted for other classes.

You will probably want to use stories from each of these categories, as suits the needs of the class and to develop different skills in pupils, e.g. learning specific vocabulary/ language structures, listening for gist understanding, consolidating previously learned language.

WHAT GENERAL QUALITIES DOES THE STORY NEED?

- There should be a good storyline.
- There should be a sense of climax to allow pupils to anticipate what happens next.
- The content of the story should be accessible to pupils, neither babyish nor too adult.
- It should be neither too long, so as to avoid losing concentration, nor too short, so as to allow audience involvement.

WHAT QUALITIES DOES THE STORY NEED FOR LANGUAGE DEVELOPMENT?

- There should be repetition of key structures to enable pupils to participate.
- The amount of new vocabulary and language structures should be limited so that pupils can remember some of the new language with a view to using it themselves rather than only understanding it.
- The language of the story, i.e. language structures and vocabulary, should suit the pupils. If you opt to adapt a story from English you can tell the story using only the language that is necessary to convey the basic message of the story. You might use the same story with more complicated language with more advanced pupils, but even then resist the temptation to add more language than is necessary.
- The illustrations should help pupils to understand the story and allow them to pass comment, often using language that is already familiar to them.

WHAT QUALITIES DOES THE STORYTELLER NEED?

OK, so you are now convinced that there is potential in using storytelling as part of the foreign language programme for your pupils. Apart from obvious skills in the foreign language, you need to possess certain qualities:

- a willingness to perform, change voices, use gestures and facial expressions, an ability to engage the audience — just as in telling a story to a class in English;
- the ability to recognise what language structures and vocabulary you have to practise with pupils prior to them hearing the story so that they can enjoy the story and not feel threatened by it;
- a good memory or the ability to ad-lib or to read and act at the same time.

Fine, you have passed those tests and you know the qualities that a story should have. Perhaps you already have some stories in mind. The next few chapters will show you how to exploit them to the full, as well as suggesting some stories which have already been used successfully by teachers as part of their foreign language programme.

1. Leading into the story

So, you have decided to go ahead. Your storytelling abilities have been perfected and you have a suitable story in mind. If not, then Chapter 5 will give you some ideas as to stories that have worked well. But where do you start?

In some cases you could launch straight into the story where the pictures, mime and gesture allow you to convey the meaning, especially if the story is already familiar to the pupils. However, some lead-up work is usually necessary and will help develop the pupils' linguistic knowledge. The amount of this lead-up work can be a little or a lot depending on the pupils' previous knowledge of the vocabulary and language structures. The decision is yours. If you wish to launch straight into the story — fine, skip this chapter and come back to it after reading Chapter 2. Even then there is so much you can do that you will need to select which of the activities you feel are appropriate for you and your class.

 ## IDENTIFYING THE KEY LANGUAGE

The first stage is to decide what language you wish to teach the pupils in advance. Let us consider some examples: *The very hungry caterpillar* and *Goldilocks.*

The key language in the *The very hungry caterpillar* is/could be food, days of the week, whereas in *Goldilocks* it could be feelings (hungry, thirsty, sad, etc), size/furniture (a big bed, a middle-sized bed, a small bed, etc), crockery/cutlery (a bowl, a spoon, etc), rooms (bedroom, kitchen, etc), the family (daddy bear, mummy bear, etc).

In both cases, you could either limit yourself to the actual language to be found in the story, e.g. not all the rooms feature in *Goldilocks,* or you could extend the language to cover that language area, although this might be best left until after the story.

 ## DEVELOPING THE KEY LANGUAGE

There are many ways of developing the key language: flashcards, overhead projector transparencies (OHTs), card games, physical games, board games, etc. Which ways you use will depend on the time you wish to devote to the language, but more importantly on whether you wish the pupils to listen, to read, to write, to speak or to practise a combination of these skills.

FLASHCARDS

Picture flashcards are a wonderful resource which can be used in so many ways. Some are commercially available, but if not the creation of home-made cards could be part of an art activity in advance of the language lesson.

The simplest and most obvious way is to show the flashcard, say the word depicted and the pupils listen in silence before they are asked to repeat. This exercise is obviously useful in providing a pronunciation model for pupils to imitate. However, as experienced teachers know, this can become somewhat boring if prolonged, with the obvious consequences for indiscipline. You can vary it with remarkable results in terms of motivation! The pupils are asked to repeat in a hushed voice, in a loud voice, slowly, quickly, with an echo, etc. They enjoy the fun, although when you plan to use *à haute voix, en voz alta, ad alta voce, laut,* it might be an idea to have warned your colleagues nearby as the pupils exercise their lungs!

Even repeating in various ways has its limitations though, so you can make it into a game. Each of the flashcards can be given a number and as the pupils hear you say the word or phrase they have to tell you the number of the corresponding flashcard. Obviously if they know the number in the foreign language, they can say it but if not, then identification using English is an acceptable alternative.

Other listen and recognise games include:

- the pupils run/point towards the correct flashcards which are stuck up around the room;
- you distribute a card to each pupil and they hold up their card when they hear the word or phrase;
- you divide the room into two halves — one TRUE and the other FALSE. You hold up a card, saying a word or phrase and the pupils have to go to the correct half of the room according to whether you said the true or false word or phrase.

Once you feel the pupils have heard the new language sufficiently, you might wish to let them see the written word, perhaps by matching labels to the flashcards. Again, it would be possible to vary this activity by making it into a true/false activity, holding a label and a flashcard and asking if the match is correct or not.

You can give pupils a picture flashcard each and ask them to arrange themselves in alphabetical order according to the first letter of each word in the foreign language.

At this stage as preparation for the story, you might be happy with simple recognition with the speaking coming later after the story. However, should you want to consolidate the new language, the following flashcard activities work well:

A guessing game — It is a matter of some puzzlement to us why pupils can be bored with flashcards and yet by making them into a guessing game, you revive their interest and all hands start to go up, but that is what tends to happen! You conceal the cards by having them facing you and you ask pupils to guess which one you are looking at. If you want to make it easier, you can offer them choices or clues as to what is on the card.

A number game — As above, you number the cards but this time you give the number and ask the pupils to say the word/phrase rather than the number.

Noughts and crosses — You have your master plan on a piece of paper, e.g. nine boxes and the names of your flashcards. You also have a corresponding plan on the board but with each box blank and the flashcards displayed at random beside the board. The pupils guess which flashcard goes where by saying the number of a box and choosing one of the flashcards. If their choice is correct according to your master plan, you award that team the flashcard and an O or X in the box on the board.

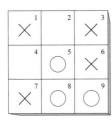

Kim's game — The flashcards are laid out or put up on the board. The pupils are required to close their eyes. You remove one card and the pupils then guess which one is missing.

THE OVERHEAD PROJECTOR

Many of the exercises above can be done using the OHP, e.g. repetition in its many forms, recognition by number, the true/false game.

Kim's game can be done on the OHP by the use of flaps or Post-its, turning off the machine and concealing one or more of the pictures before turning it back on. Many of these ideas are outlined in Pathfinder 15: *Improve your image: the effective use of the OHP* (CILT, 1992).

The OHTs can be easily created using commercial materials such as the Mary Glasgow Timesavers series (see Resources p36). Again, the pupils could perhaps create the necessary drawings as an art activity. They enjoy creating OHTs and seeing their work projected onto the screen.

CARD GAMES

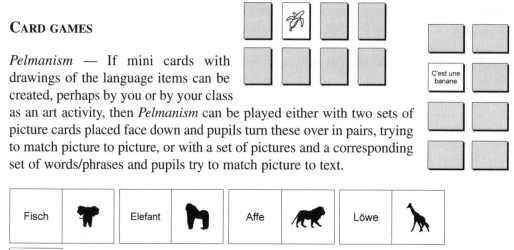

Pelmanism — If mini cards with drawings of the language items can be created, perhaps by you or by your class as an art activity, then *Pelmanism* can be played either with two sets of picture cards placed face down and pupils turn these over in pairs, trying to match picture to picture, or with a set of pictures and a corresponding set of words/phrases and pupils try to match picture to text.

Fisch		Elefant		Affe		Löwe	

Dominoes — In a similar way, picture and text cards can be created and dominoes can be played with pupils matching picture to picture or text to text.

Snap — You can create multiple sets via the photocopier and pupils can play snap.

Happy families — This game can be used to allow pupils to practise the new language, e.g. in the key language for *Goldilocks*, the four families could be furniture pertaining to four rooms in the house or it is possible to practise the size variations using cards for the table, chair, bed, bowl.

Word forming — Cards of letters can also be used for groups of pupils to form the new words on their desks or to label flashcards. This activity can be made into a competitive game by introducing a time limit.

Miniflashcard games — MiniFlashcard Games produce mini cards which can be used for many of the above games and in many more ways, which are outlined in the suggestions accompanying the cards.

BOARD GAMES

Snakes and ladders — The commercial board game *Snakes and ladders* can be used to develop any language area. As a pupil lands on a snake or a ladder he or she takes a card from a pile of created picture cards related to the story, e.g. fruits. If he or she gets it right then he or she goes up or down as appropriate.

Home-made games — A simple home-made version could easily be created using simple desk top publishing — a board with 30 squares numbered. A number of squares could have cards placed on them, e.g. for *Goldilocks* you could have cards of furniture on two squares, family cards on another two and so on. If a pupil lands on the square, the card is turned over and if the pupil is correct then he or she advances three places, if wrong he or she goes back two places.

PHYSICAL GAMES

Physical games too can be used to help the pupils to recognise and to practise the language before the story. There are countless games which you will know from infant classes, PE activities, etc, but here are some which have been used successfully in the primary schools teaching a foreign language.

Bring me . . . — Pupils are divided into groups and given sets of cards with pictures of the new language. You call out *'Bring me . . .'*, e.g. in the case of *The very hungry caterpillar* '*Bring mir zwei Äpfel und eine Birne*'. One of each group runs to you with the requested cards and the first to arrive scores a point for that group.

The four corners game — This can be played with a picture or text card being placed in each corner. You ask the pupils to choose a corner. You then turn over a card from your matching set of cards. Those pupils who chose that corner are eliminated and sit down while the others return to the centre and carry out a forfeit which relates to language being learned or revises language before the game is restarted.

The fruit bowl game — You sit all the pupils in a circle and go round the circle giving each one a 'name' or a card, e.g. you are an apple, you are a pear, you a plum, etc. You want approximately three or four pupils with the same 'label' or card. You call out one of the labels, e.g. apple, and all those who have that label are required to change seat. You take one of the vacated chairs if possible — yes, don't get caught out and be left in the middle — and one of the pupils is left in the middle to call out the next label. You also want to have a collective word which means they all have to change, e.g. fruit in this case. This is a great game which pupils really enjoy and can be used to develop any linguistic area.

Miming — Pupils can mime or play charades, e.g. if the key language area was animals as in *Dear zoo* or in *Mr Gumpy's outing* they could mime the movement of the animals. They can play charades and try to convey the meaning for key language associated with most stories.

OTHER IDEAS

Bingo — Picture bingo is a great way to practise recognition of the new language. It can be easily created by pupils doing simple drawings.

I spy — The pupils can practise the new language by playing the game '*I spy something beginning with the letter . . .*'

Feelie bag — For some language areas it might be possible to use real objects, e.g. fruit, clothes, classroom objects. One item is placed secretly in a bag. A pupil is asked to feel in the bag and guess what the object is. Alternatively, several items, for which the pupils already know the names, are placed in the bag and you call out the name of one of them. The pupil has to feel in the bag and find that object.

Listen and draw — You name items which the children have been practising and they make a quick drawing of the item. This is particularly useful for personal descriptions when you can describe a drawing and they have to draw the description. You can then compare the pupils' versions with the original drawing.

A variation of this idea can be where a card screen is placed between pairs or groups of pupils and they give each other descriptions and both draw to fit the descriptions.

The shopping game — This is a memory game which can be played quickly round the class to practise new vocabulary. One pupil starts by saying, e.g. for clothing '*In my bag I have a tie*'. The next pupil repeats that and adds another item of clothing and so on.

And finally

Time will have flown past . . . you would not believe that a story could take so much time and give the pupils so much fun, even if you selected only some of these ideas. Now it is time for the story itself . . .

2.   Are you sitting comfortably?

*Il était
une fois . . .*

Well, the day has arrived. The key language has been developed
and you have your book, flashcards or OHTs ready.

 TELLING THE STORY FOR THE FIRST TIME

You will want to let the pupils hear the story for the first time in its entirety using lots of
gesture, mime, pointing to key parts, etc. Pupils will be enthralled as they discover a new
story or as they hear a familiar story but in the foreign language.

Before they have tried them, some primary teachers have been a little concerned about
the traditional fairy tales being seen as babyish for ten-year-olds. They have listened to
others and have been persuaded to give them a try. Others have commented on the
excitement among older pupils too. The fact that it is in another language is OK by these
grown-up ten-year-olds! They have a superior feeling because they can understand so
much in the foreign language.

 INVOLVING THE PUPILS

CHORUSING

You can take the pupils through the story with them chorusing after you key parts of the
text. You could vary this activity in the same way as with flashcards and have the pupils
chorusing loudly, in a whisper, slowly, etc.

MIMING

You can encourage the pupils to mime along with you to associate the text with certain
actions or sounds, e.g. the actions or sounds of animals in the story *Mr Gumpy's outing*
or the illnesses in the story *Simon is ill* or the emotions in *Goldilocks* — '*Boucles d'Or
est triste . . .*' You will see how this is done with the story of *Mr Gumpy's outing* in
Chapter 6.

RECOGNISING KEY LANGUAGE

Distribute cards of either key language, e.g. food in *The very hungry caterpillar,* or parts
of the story to individual pupils. As you retell the story with/without the aid of visuals

the pupils show their card to the rest of the class as they hear the corresponding language. This can be extended sometimes to involve the pupils more in mime, e.g. in *Goldilocks* the pupils can listen for the emotions, the appropriate card held up and the other pupils encouraged to mime a corresponding action.

SENTENCE COMPLETION

As you retell the story you encourage the pupils to complete sentences, e.g. in the story of *Mr Gumpy's outing* you start off the question '*Est-ce que je . . . (peux venir aussi)?*' or the sentence '*Et le . . . monte dans le bateau*', gradually reducing the amount of language you provide as a starter as the pupils become more familiar with the text. In the story of *The very hungry caterpillar* you start off the list of foods it eats and encourage the pupils to list the remainder as you point to them. In the story *Simon is ill* the pupils guess what is wrong for that day of the week. You can coax more language out of the pupils, e.g. by offering alternatives and encouraging the pupils to choose the appropriate phrase or sentence.

MEMORY GAMES

Lists can provide excellent fun in terms of memory games and chorusing, e.g. food in *The very hungry caterpillar*, animals in the case of *Mr Gumpy's outing*, members of the family in the story of *The little elephant* who wants a nose like his dad, mum, brother, sister. The pupils try to remember which item is next on the list before you turn the page or show the next card.

If you wish to play a memory game and need to hide parts of the pictures then Post-it sticky notes are a simple and effective way of doing so.

Some teachers use the OHP to tell the story, hiding parts of pictures with card flaps.

It is also possible to use overlays, i.e. an additional transparency on top of another one which can be removed or brought into play. In one memorable case in Spanish a primary teacher used a version of *Little Red Riding Hood* where in different pictures the wolf was hiding in different places. The children quickly picked up on the warning that the wolf was behind — '*Cuidado, el lobo está detrás*', followed by the question where, '*¿Dónde?*' with the appropriate answer. The teacher then made this into a fun memory game by retelling the story, having removed the overlay featuring the wolf and asking the pupils where the wolf was. Their obvious concern for *Little Red Riding Hood* became evident as they chorused out in the tree — *'En el arbol'*, or whatever answer was appropriate.

Another wonderful example was the story of *The enormous turnip* (see p14) where a new overlay was brought in to represent each new person in the line who was trying to pull the giant turnip from the ground. The pupils became very involved in listing each new person who joined the line.

CHECKING COMPREHENSION

As you tell the story you might wish to ask questions about key parts. This might be done in English or you might ask in the foreign language with the pupil replying in English, e.g. *'Qu'est-ce que c'est un cornichon?'*, giving clues such as *'C'est vert comme un concombre'*, with the pupil suggesting *'Is it a gherkin, miss?'*. Another way to check comprehension would be for both the question/answer to be done in the foreign language. As always, much depends on the abilities of your pupils.

Although you might wish to check comprehension, it will be important not to interrupt the flow of the story too much nor to take all the fun out of it by constant questioning. The pupils often give a running commentary in English as the story is being told and they look for reassurance that they are understanding it. This is fine; all you have to do is nod to give this reassurance. If the pupils are wrong, you could rephrase or repeat the sentence or phrase that has not been understood.

PRACTISING KEY SOUNDS

The story might contain certain key sounds which pupils could practise in the context of the story, imitating a correct model which you provide live with the pupils repeating after you. The sounds vary from story to story and you might wish to pick out the key sound(s) you wish to practise, whether an *U* sound in French, the Italian *Ci* or the Spanish *J*. In Chapter 6 you will see how the story of *Mr Gumpy's outing* allows for work on the sounds *ch: chat, chien, chèvre, cochon* and *au: Beauregard, eau, chaud, bateau, aussi.*

The next stage

You have told the story. Maybe you want to leave it at that but there is much more potential to develop the language of the story itself — through reading, writing, listening and speaking, as well as the potential for enjoyment through games, activities and drama.

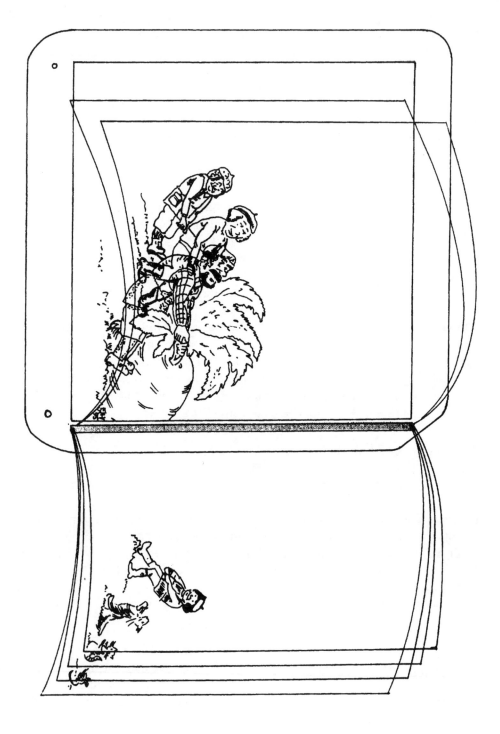

Use of the OHP for *The enormous turnip*

14

3.   Developing the story

In Chapter 1 we gave ideas as to how you can develop some of the key language in the lead-up to the story. You can now extend those ideas to the actual language of the story itself, going beyond only the key words and phrases and developing the 'surround' language also, thus giving your pupils greater chunks of language, longer phrases and sentences and using these in the context of the story. You can also show your pupils how these language structures work and how to reuse this language in other contexts.

Also in Chapter 1 we suggested that you might wish to extend a language area of the story, e.g. in the story of *Goldilocks* adding in other rooms of the house and not limiting yourself to those that feature in the story. You might prefer to leave that extension until after the story. The choice is yours depending on time factors, how the class has coped with the language to date, i.e. can they take any more at present and of course the level of interest in the class.

DEVELOPING THE LANGUAGE

The focus is different. At this stage you are possibly developing the extended language of the story, e.g. sentences such as '*Elle remarque trois tables: une grande table*', etc, rather than simply the names of the furniture on their own. Alternatively, you are possibly going beyond the key language for that language area, e.g. not simply the furniture mentioned in *Goldilocks* but adding other items of furniture. Or indeed you might be going to do both. Whatever you decide, many of the principles outlined in Chapter 1 still apply. Flashcard work, card games, physical games, board games and OHTs can all be used. However, there are some ways which have been particularly successful after the story, so let us consider those in more detail here.

MATCHING KEY LANGUAGE TO ASPECTS OF THE STORY

- Pupils are asked to identify some language from the story. The pupils are given cards of the main characters/objects/animals or perhaps events in the story. You read out phrases or sentences from the story and they hold up the card of the character who said that or the appropriate animal or the corresponding object or whatever.

- You involve the pupils in producing the language by showing them cards relating to the story and perhaps starting off a phrase or a sentence associated with that card encouraging them to complete what you are saying.

- Alternatively, you give clues relating to the characters. As you do so, the pupils try to identify which character it is and hold up the corresponding card, perhaps repeating the key language at the same time.

- Depending on the pupils' abilities you might also engage them in question and answer about some of the characters or events in the story.

MATCHING PICTURE TO TEXT

- You provide the pupils with picture cards of the story with corresponding cards which contain the text and ask the pupils to match the two sets. Whereas in Chapter 1 this was seen in the context of key words, at this stage you could extend the text — perhaps a phrase or even two or three sentences.

- The two sets of cards can also be used to play *Pelmanism,* with the pupils being required to read out the text card.

- The text cards can be used with you reading out or playing a cassette with parts of the story and the pupils being required to find the corresponding text and then perhaps also to read the text aloud.

- Two sets (picture/text) can also be used to play *Portholes*. To do this you make two strips of card back to back. On one strip you have picture cards and on the other you have the text. Using a punch, you create holes through both sides of the strips. A pupil reads out one of the pieces of text. The other pupil looks at the picture strip, identifies which picture belongs to that text and pushes a pencil through the 'porthole' to show his or her choice.

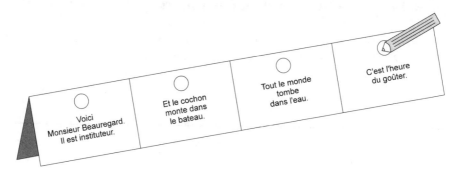

LISTEN AND DRAW

The pupils hear details from the story, e.g. in the story of *Goldilocks* — *'Boucles d'Or habite une jolie maison dans la forêt'*, and are asked to draw a picture to match. These can be used to add to a wall frieze depicting the story which can also have a corresponding text added.

You can extend this activity. The pupils are given an A4 sheet of paper which they fold into six or eight boxes. They listen to a phrase and they draw a corresponding picture, e.g. *'Voici Boucles d'Or devant sa maison. Elle cueille des fleurs.'* Each of the pictures gives the main events of the story. Pupils are then involved in a group activity giving each other instructions to colour in their drawings. Once this has been done, they are given a sheet with the text you used for the listening activity. They choose the correct phrases, cut them out and glue them to the correct pictures, thus creating their own mini version of the story.

SEQUENCING

Provide the pupils with sets of mini picture cards. As you retell the story, they place the cards in the correct order.

Alternatively, provide the pupils with the written text, with or without the pictures, cut up into strips, and ask them to put the story strips into the correct order, either as they hear the story as a language recognition game or from memory.

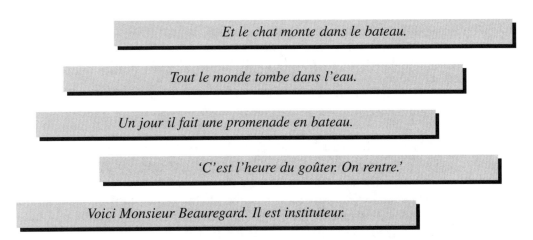

Et le chat monte dans le bateau.

Tout le monde tombe dans l'eau.

Un jour il fait une promenade en bateau.

'C'est l'heure du goûter. On rentre.'

Voici Monsieur Beauregard. Il est instituteur.

Depending on your pupils' word processing skills you can also provide them with the text out of order and ask them to rearrange it by 'cutting and pasting' text.

STORYTELLING AND DRAMA

The story can lead to a lot of exciting drama work related to the language after the retelling of the story.

THE PUPILS BECOME CHARACTERS

The pupils take the role of individual characters in the story and are asked to provide the dialogue for those characters as the story is retold. For example in the story of *The little elephant* each pupil is given a role and gives advice to the little elephant, e.g. the pupil taking the role of the giraffe tells him/her '*Va chez M le Lion*', the pupil taking the role of the lion tells him/her '*Va chez M le Singe*' and so on.

THE PUPILS MIME ACTIONS

For some stories pupils mime the actions as they hear the story, e.g. as they hear each animal in the story *Dear zoo* they attempt a mime representing that particular animal, e.g. the trunk of an elephant, the height of a giraffe. It is also possible for them to link the language of the story to noises, e.g. the noises which animals make.

To take another example, *The mixed-up chameleon,* the pupils mime the animal that the chameleon wants to be like, e.g. as beautiful as a flamingo, swim like a fish, run like a deer, etc.

CREATING A SCRIPT

The story can be turned into a playlet. The pupils might be able to do this with a little help or, just as you did with the story itself, you might provide them with a playlet version out of order and ask them to do this as a sequencing activity. Having done so, they then act out their script.

The playlet allows the pupils to use language from the story and also other language which they know and which helps them to retell the story, i.e. they choose simple familiar language to convey the message. To take the example of *Hansel and Gretel*, the pupils can use familiar language like *sit down, stand up, come here*, etc to link the story. This language is not part of the story but is familiar to pupils and enables them to retell the story in a straightforward way. They do not need to rely so much on the new language of the story.

The script used for the playlet may be one specifically created, thus developing the pupils' creative abilities. Alternatively, it can be the original script which has been memorised, thus developing the pupils' memorisation skills.

Another successful way which has been seen is where the pupils create their own script by choosing appropriate speech bubbles and sticking these into their exercise book. The story can also be acted out or read to another class.

The story also provides opportunities for playlets from incidents which are part of the story but which do not feature largely in it, e.g. the three bears as they are out on their walk or the conversation between Hansel and Gretel as they overhear what their stepfather is plotting. These scenes allow the pupils to use familiar language in an imaginative way and competition between different groups working on the same scene increases motivation.

BRINGING THE STORY TO LIFE

You can enhance the drama scene by creating props. This can be done in English but perhaps instructions to colour in, etc, might be given through the foreign language. You can make animal masks for the story *Dear zoo,* an elephant puppet for the story of *The little elephant* or animals for the story of *The lion hunt.* Art and Craft work is thus linked to the story, as indeed many other aspects of the primary curriculum can be. That is another stage and it is developed in the next chapter.

4. Linking the story to aspects of the curriculum

There are a variety of ways of dealing with a story as part of the foreign language programme for a class. Much will depend on the amount of time that you want to devote to the story; you may be surprised at how much you can do with a story, as we have seen in previous chapters and as you will see from the example given in Chapter 6. Look to the potential of the story, look at the language that can be learned from it rather than moving quickly to the next 'topic' in the foreign language programme.

 THE STORY AS THE BASIS FOR DEVELOPING SPECIFIC LANGUAGE STRUCTURES/VOCABULARY

For example, *The very hungry caterpillar* is used to introduce various items of food, after which pupils are taught to express likes/dislikes of these items of food, before moving to more items of food and other activities related to food. These activities can move beyond the foreign language by their immediate relevance to other aspects of the curriculum.

- Daily diet: keeping a record of what is eaten daily and putting this under headings of healthy/not healthy, sweet/savoury, etc. The gains from such an activity can be taken much further than developing vocabulary in the foreign language.
- Café/restaurant scene: acting out the scene, learning how to lay a table and act in a restaurant, understanding prices, taking turns in a conversation, as well as making the menus and other props necessary for the scene.
- Shopping for food: understanding prices, creating shopping lists for a specific meal — often a picnic or birthday party, acting out the scene are valid components in the foreign language programme as well as contributing to skills to be developed elsewhere in the curriculum.
- Simple cooking: recipes in the foreign language, usually from books specifically written for children with appropriate illustrations, or adapting familiar recipes from English have both been used successfully. The skills of following instructions, weighing/mixing, cleaning up have been developed through the foreign language. Much of the language itself has been simple commands: *mesurez, mélangez, ajoutez, regardez, faites attention,* etc.

THE STORY AS PART OF THE OVERALL LANGUAGE AREA

For example, a story such as *The snowman* could be one element of work being done on Christmas. The story provides a focus for language development through the many activities surrounding it and other activities in the foreign language continue with the Christmas theme, build on and extend previously acquired skills in the foreign language as well as calling on skills acquired outwith and relevant beyond the foreign language.

Examples of such activities might include:

 a craft activity to make cardboard figures of Santa Claus by measuring, cutting and sticking as appropriate;

hearing about how Christmas is celebrated in the country/countries where the language is spoken;

 creating a Christmas mobile through a listen and draw activity;

some Christmas carols/songs, to add a cultural dimension as well as an exercise in pronunciation and in musical skills.

 ## THE STORY AS PART OF THE OVERALL THEME OF THE CLASS

For example, one teacher linked the telling of the stories *Dear Greenpeace* and *My friend whale* in German to the overall theme of conservation, covered in other curricular areas, namely language, maths, environmental studies, creative/aesthetic skills, RE/moral education.

KEY IDEA - PROTECTION OF ANIMALS: ACTIVITIES

Activities to develop language skills	Activities to develop maths skills	Activities to develop environmental studies skills
Quiz — How green are you? Write letters to WWF, Greenpeace, etc. Wordsearch/crosswords of conservation vocabulary. Cloze procedure on ozone layer facts. Creative writing — mud slides, newspaper articles written about oil spills — leading to poems written about oiled birds. Debate on pollution — read *Greenwatch* — 'Sad song of the whale'. Pollution 'shape' poem. Research in library to produce fact file on endangered species. Reporting on oil/pollution experiments.	Litter pollution survey — graph results. Read results and trends from graphs, charts, tables.	Investigate food chains and webs. Draw diagrams of photosynthesis. Investigate decomposers and natural waste to lead to natural recycling. Study greenhouse effect, discuss, draw diagrams. Investigate causes of ozone depletion. Research ways to reduce damage. Use atlas to find rainforest areas. Research plants, animals, products of rainforest. Experiments to show properties/effects of oil use. Subject seeds and seedlings to acid rain — experiments with vinegar solution.

KEY IDEA — PROTECTION OF ANIMALS: ACTIVITIES

Activities to develop aesthetic skills	Activities to develop RE and moral skills	German topic areas involved
Design 'Save the rainforest' posters.	*Genesis* 1,2 — creation discussion of man's place on earth and responsibility for it.	Names of endangered species — descriptions of animals + their habitat.
Draw pencil drawing of oiled birds from observation of pictures.	Design a perfect world. Write about how you would look after it.	Creation of slogans — 'Save our . . .' , 'Help our . . .'
Design a T-shirt with a conservation motto/picture.	Write a prayer for the world.	Design posters/T-shirts with conservation message.
Design and make a 'Green' board game with full instructions.	Discuss moral issues in rainforest destruction — global implications.	Likes and dislikes — eating habits, means of travel.
		Reading + listening — *Mein Freund Wal, Dear Greenpeace.*
		Wall display of *Dear Greenpeace* and habitats correctly labelled.

Margaret Hutcheon, Mosstowie Primary School, Grampian Region

PROTECTION OF ANIMALS: German language programme

Vocabulary	names of endangered species both wild and tame — definite article and colour coding to reinforce gender.
Descriptive language	relating to these animals — consolidation of previously learned language plus some new words — dangerous, tame, wild, fierce — build up fact files on animals.
Countryside language	to describe habitat of animals, consolidating from previous theme describing Mosstowie. New words — jungle, mountains, desert, plains, treetops.
Grammar	position — in the tree tops, on the plains, among the mountains.
Likes and dislikes	use of *gern* for eating habits and favourite foods.
Reading and Listening	story of *Mein Freund Wal* and *Dear Greenpeace* (in German). German assistant to tape the stories — cloze passages/answer questions.
Art and Craft	wall display of *Dear Greenpeace* and habitats of other animals labelled. Design posters/T-shirts with a conservation message.

 ## TO LINK OR NOT TO LINK . . .

Whether or not you choose to link the theme of the foreign language to the theme of the class, using a story develops skills which you, the teacher, will want to develop in the pupils' curriculum. A look at some of the activities in Chapter 6 shows that from the story of *Mr Gumpy's outing* skills were being developed in:

- listening;
- sequencing text/ matching text to picture;
- drama;
- craft activities;
- memorising text;
- singing and creating verses for the song.

All of these activities would be appropriate in English; choosing to do them in the foreign language adds another dimension to them and shows the potential offered by opting for the framework of a story to bind them together. It is also an economy in time: you are practising and developing the foreign language at the same time as allowing the pupils to learn from activities which you would do in any case in class.

5. Some of the stories that have been successfully used to date

No story comes with a guarantee of success since so much depends on you, the story-teller, your class and what you do with the story. However, the ideas given in the previous chapters should set you on the road to success, the next question being what type of story you might use. You will no doubt be familiar with many stories which would work, either because of their appeal to pupils, because they would link in to the work of your class or because they are particular favourites of yours and you know that your enthusiasm will transfer to your audience. If you know exactly the type of stories that you can use, skip to the next chapter!

The following list is by no means exhaustive — nor should it be seen as publicity for specific books! They are, however, stories which have been used successfully and which might guide you in your choice. For each story mentioned there will be many which serve the same purpose and which you will already have in school — use them, tell your colleagues about them and begin exchanging their successes with yours, not to mention exchanging the 'package' for the story, thus economising on preparation time!

As we said in the introduction, there are three categories of stories:

- traditional tales or stories that will most likely be familiar to pupils;
- stories which link well to a particular theme (and which also might be traditional tales);
- stories which have been created or adapted for a class to tie in to a theme or to develop a specific language point.

 TRADITIONAL TALES

The enormous turnip

The language is very simple and repetitive and there is considerable scope for acting out the story and giving 'speaking parts' to a number of pupils. There is also scope for imagination in adding more characters to the tale.

Snow White

This story can be told at various levels, ranging from very simple language to more complex and detailed language. It offers scope for describing characters in terms of physical appearance, character, clothes and interests and has been successfully turned into a playlet on several occasions.

Goldilocks

The level of language can vary considerably here, moving from a restricted, factual telling of the story to involving pupils in describing characters, the house and furnishings and stating what lesson can be learned from the story.

The Emperor's new clothes

Once again this story can be told in a restricted, factual form or by allowing pupils to give details of the clothes worn by characters. The story also allows for repetition in the statements made by several of the characters.

Hansel and Gretel

This story allows pupils to describe the characters and the house of the witch and can easily be turned into a playlet, accompanied by traditional lullabies.

The Pied Piper of Hamelin

Apart from the telling of the basic story, there is scope here for imaginative adaptation to reinforce the vocabulary for buildings in a town, prepositions, as well as descriptive language for the rats and the piper. Musical talent can be called upon to invent the tune that the piper played.

Three little pigs

This is a story with a lot of repetition in language and an easily memorised rhyme, thus encouraging pupil participation — and leading to some interesting craft work building the various type of houses!

Stories from series which are designed for reluctant readers, e.g. Wellington Square, Skyways, Bookbus, Sunshine Books are appropriate for pupils in terms of maturity, with some stories dealing with specific issues, e.g. bullying, greed, as well as having good illustrations which encourage imaginative additions to the story from teacher and pupils.

 STORIES THAT LINK TO PARTICULAR THEMES

The snowman — **Raymond Briggs**

This story links to a Christmas theme, it is text-free, allowing text at any level and inviting participation and suggestions from pupils. The animated film has been successfully used with teachers adding their own text.

The huge bag of worries — **Virginia Ironside**

This is an RSPCC book, part of a personal and social development programme in schools to encourage pupils to talk to an adult if they have worries. The language is sufficiently simple to convey the message in the foreign language, thus making the foreign language part of the curriculum. Some pupils wrote a slogan for the story in the foreign language, others added speech bubbles to the picture that they had drawn depicting a scene from the book.

My friend whale + Dear Greenpeace — **Simon James**

Both books have links to a theme on conservation, with language that can be easily adapted into the foreign language and understood through the illustrations. *Dear Greenpeace* can be used to develop some letter-writing skills in the foreign language.

The very hungry caterpillar — **Eric Carle**

This story can be used as an introduction to names of food in the foreign language or as part of an overall theme on food.

Mr Gumpy's outing — **John Burningham**

This story links to a theme on animals, develops commands and asking permission and has scope for drama and for pupils adding different animals to the story, along with suggestions as to what Mr Gumpy tells them not to do.

Dear zoo — **Rod Clark**

This book links to a theme on animals and adjectives associated with certain animals — and has scope for adding different animals and the reasons why they were sent back to the zoo or were kept as pets.

The mixed-up chameleon — **Eric Carle**

This is a story with a moral and links to a theme on animals, associating animals with certain attributes/characteristics. Further wishes which the chameleon might have had can be added or pupils can create a similar story about themselves.

The monster pot plant — **Diana Webb**

This is a modern *Jack and the beanstalk* with humour and scope for drama.

That fat cat — **Michael Eltham**

This is a variation of *The enormous turnip*, with a lot of repetitive language and with scope for drama and additional characters.

The jolly postman — **Janet & Allan Ahlberg**

The rhyme will be lost in the foreign language, but the contents of the letters for the characters (from traditional tales) is excellent for anticipating what comes next and can serve to develop skills in letter-writing in the foreign language.

Willy and Hugh + Willy the champ — **Anthony Browne**

Both books have a moral (e.g. the value of friendship) and the illustrations allow pupils to comment on the characters and the action of the story. There is scope for predicting what happens next and for direct speech/drama.

The owl who was afraid of the dark — **Jill Tomlinson**

This story repeats structures, thus allowing pupils to participate and to predict what happens next. There is scope for imaginative additions to the story, still following the same pattern.

ADAPTED/HOME-MADE STORIES

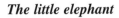

The little elephant

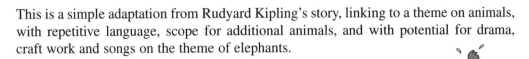

This is a simple adaptation from Rudyard Kipling's story, linking to a theme on animals, with repetitive language, scope for additional animals, and with potential for drama, craft work and songs on the theme of elephants.

Simon is ill

This story deals with the variety of illnesses which Simon pretends to have each day of the week, repeating structures, modal verbs and using commands as Mother tells him what he should do, namely to go to school! There is a moral too: Simon is really ill at the weekend.

Zack, the space-girl

There are similarities to *The little elephant* and *Dear zoo* as a space-girl tries to find a home on earth, the location varying with the pupils' surroundings. The story introduces buildings in a town and adjectives as to why Zack cannot stay there. Her choice of habitat can be the school — or wherever the pupils choose.

The lion hunt

This is an action story, with pupils repeating what the teacher (or a pupil leading the hunt) says. There is scope for adding other obstacles which have to be overcome on the hunt and for creating suitable mimes.

The potato family

This is a variation of *The enormous turnip,* with structures repeated and allowing scope for additional characters — and what the family does with the potato once it is harvested.

6. Theory into practice: *Mr Gumpy's outing*

Mr Gumpy's outing by John Burningham (Picture Puffins) has been a great success in schools. It works well for several reasons:

- the illustrations are excellent and offer scope for the pupils to add their own comments;
- the language is simple and repetitive and pupils can join in;
- it focuses on certain language points, namely asking permission and giving commands;
- it links well to a theme on animals and leads easily to craft work, songs and games;
- it has scope for being turned into a playlet by pupils.

The text can be easily translated, using language that is perhaps more simple than the English but which still tells the same story and which concentrates on language that will be familiar to pupils and in which they can see patterns. The example offered below is in French but the same principle applies to any language. You will note that we have changed the name of the character, concentrating on the positive and pleasant side of his nature. We also gave him a job as a teacher, to convey the message that he is a friend and to avoid the suggestion that the children (and animals) went on an outing with a stranger.

Basic text	Exploitation of text by teacher
Voici Monsieur Beauregard. Il est instituteur.	Pupils describe Mr Gumpy.
Voici son bateau et sa maison. Il habite près de la rivière.	Pupils describe his house, where it might be.
Un jour il fait une promenade en bateau. 'Bonjour, Monsieur Beauregard, est-ce qu'on peut venir aussi?' demandent les enfants. *'Oui, mais ne vous disputez pas', répond Monsieur Beauregard.* *Et les enfants montent dans le bateau. Dans le bateau il y a maintenant Monsieur Beauregard et les enfants.*	Pupils name the children, give them ages, etc. Gesture to convey 'don't argue'. Start list of who is in the boat.

Basic text	Exploitation of text by teacher
'Bonjour, Monsieur Beauregard, est-ce que je peux venir aussi?' demande le lapin. *'Oui, mais ne saute pas', répond Monsieur Beauregard. Et le lapin monte dans le bateau. Dans le bateau il y a maintenant Monsieur Beauregard, les enfants et le lapin.*	Pupils guess the animal, describe rabbit, mime to convey 'don't jump', question about who has a rabbit at home. Continue list of who is in the boat.
'Bonjour, Monsieur Beauregard, est-ce que je peux venir aussi?' demande le chat. *'Oui, mais ne chasse pas le lapin', répond Monsieur Beauregard.* *Et le chat monte dans le bateau. Dans le bateau il y a maintenant . . .*	Same as with rabbit. Pupils join in with cat asking Mr Gumpy. Mime 'don't chase the rabbit'. Continue with list of who is in the boat.
'Bonjour, Monsieur Beauregard, est-ce que je peux venir aussi?' demande le chien. *'Oui, mais ne tourmente pas le chat', répond Monsieur Beauregard.* *Et le chien monte dans le bateau. Dans le bateau il y a maintenant . . .*	Same as with cat. Mime to convey 'don't annoy the cat'. Continue the list of who is in the boat.
'Bonjour, Monsieur Beauregard, est-ce que je peux venir aussi?' demande le cochon. *'Oui, mais ne fais pas l'idiot', répond Monsieur Beauregard.* *Et le cochon monte dans le bateau. Dans le bateau il y a maintenant . . .*	Same as with dog. Mime to convey 'don't play the fool'. Continue with the list of who is in the boat.
'Bonjour, Monsieur Beauregard, est-ce que je peux venir aussi?' demande le mouton. *'Oui, mais ne fais pas de bruit', répond Monsieur Beauregard.* *Et le mouton monte dans le bateau. Dans le bateau il y a maintenant . . .*	Same as with pig. Mime to convey 'don't make a noise'. Continue with list of who is in the boat.

Basic text	Exploitation of text by teacher
'Bonjour, Monsieur Beauregard, est-ce qu'on peut venir aussi?' demandent les poules. *'Oui, mais ne battez pas des ailes', répond Monsieur Beauregard.* *Et les poules montent dans le bateau. Dans le bateau il y a maintenant . . .*	Same as with sheep. Mime to convey 'don't flap your wings'. Continue with the list of who is in the boat.
'Bonjour, Monsieur Beauregard, est-ce que je peux venir aussi?' demande la vache. *'Oui, mais ne bouge pas trop', répond Monsieur Beauregard.* *Et la vache monte dans le bateau. Dans le bateau il y a maintenant . . .*	Same as with hens. Mime to convey 'don't move about'. Continue with list of who is in the boat.
'Bonjour, Monsieur Beauregard, est-ce que je peux venir aussi?' demande la chèvre. *'Oui, mais ne donne pas de coups de patte', répond Monsieur Beauregard.* *Et la chèvre monte dans le bateau. Dans le bateau il y a maintenant . . .*	Same as with cow. Mime to convey 'don't kick'. Continue with list of who is in the boat.
Tout va bien pendant quelques moments. Mais . . . *la chèvre donne des coups de patte,* *la vache bouge trop,* *les poules battent des ailes,* *le mouton fait du bruit,* *le cochon fait l'idiot,* *le chien tourmente le chat,* *le chat chasse le lapin,* *le lapin saute,* *les enfants se disputent . . . et le bateau chavire. Tout le monde tombe dans l'eau.*	Pupils to name the animals in the boat and mime what each one is doing on hearing the appropriate part of the text.

Basic text	Exploitation of text by teacher
Heureusement Monsieur Beauregard, la chèvre, la vache, les poules, le mouton, le cochon, le chien, le chat, le lapin et les enfants nagent bien. 'C'est l'heure du goûter. On rentre,' dit Monsieur Beauregard.	Pupils to name animals as they walk across the field. Ask what time tea time is. Pupils give their suggestions.
Hmm, c'est délicieux!	Ask what is on the table, discuss food, likes and dislikes, act out scene.
'Bonne nuit,' dit Monsieur Beauregard. 'A la prochaine fois!' 'Bonne nuit et merci beaucoup, Monsieur Beauregard', disent les enfants.	

PREPARATION FOR TELLING THE STORY

You may want to prepare the pupils well for the story, in which case the following suggestions will be relevant. You may prefer to use the story to teach the vocabulary, in which case you will need to spend longer working on the vocabulary around the story and tell/retell the story on several occasions.

Here are some ideas, details of which were given in Chapter 1:

* use flashcards of the animals for oral recognition;
* play *The four corners game* with names of animals — and introduce some of the commands as forfeits;
* mime movements of animals as used in story;
* use cards of the animals for *Pelmanism:* picture to picture, word to picture;
* use cards of animals for dominoes: picture to picture, word to picture;
* play *I spy* with animals.

AFTER THE INITIAL TELLING OF THE STORY

There is so much that you can do, depending on the amount of time that you want to spend on the story. The following suggestions, many of which are explained in Chapter 3 in much greater detail, are not exhaustive, but they show that the story could dictate the foreign language programme for a very long time. You could choose only a few; even then the scope for language development is considerable.

- Tell the story again, with pupils having roles, e.g. greeting Mr Gumpy, asking if they can come — perhaps with certain pupils being given the part of certain animals.
- Listen and draw group activity: pupils draw characters from instructions to create a frieze of story (e.g. *Monsieur Beauregard porte un veston bleu, un chapeau vert, etc*).
- Play *Jacques a dit*, using commands from story in the positive form, then introduce the negative form.
- Play *The four corners game* with the corners labelled in the negative commands and the forfeits being from the commands given (in the positive form).
- *Pelmanism:* match command to animal.
- Label the animals on the frieze with the instructions that Mr Gumpy gave them.
- Work on sounds from story to add to a sound bank, e.g. *ch*: *chat, chien, chèvre, cochon; au: Beauregard, eau, chaud, bateau, aussi.*
- Make masks, either as a 'listen and do' or 'read and do' activity, to represent the animals.
- Tell the story again, with each animal asking permission to come and someone taking the role of Mr Gumpy, and the animals obeying his instructions. The story should now be in the form of a playlet. You might want to add more animals to involve more pupils — e.g. *le serpent, ne crache pas; la grenouille, ne saute pas; le singe, ne grimpe pas sur nous.*
- *'A table'*: drama from the conversations at the table when the group has tea, using masks made previously.
- Create a song from a familiar tune, e.g. from *The twelve days of Christmas*, using the masks created above or pictures of the animals:

1. *Monsieur Beauregard fait une promenade en bateau,*
   Monsieur Beauregard fait une promenade en bateau.
2. *Monsieur Beauregard fait une promenade en bateau,*
   Monsieur Beauregard, les petits enfants, font une promenade en bateau.
3. *Monsieur Beauregard fait une promenade en bateau,*
   Monsieur Beauregard, les petits enfants, un lapin gris, font une promenade en bateau.
4. As above, add *un chat mignon.*

5. As 4, add *un chien brun.*
6. As 5, add *un cochon rose.*
7. As 6, add *un mouton blanc.*
8. As 7, add *deux poules méchantes.*
9. As 8, add *une vache nerveuse.*
10. As 9, add *une chèvre jaune.*
    Et plouf! ils tombent dans l'eau!

AND WHERE TO NOW?

You may want to deal with another story on the theme of animals to develop the language from *Monsieur Beauregard*. If so, the following three might be of interest:

- *Old Macdonald had a farm* — work on animal noises;
- *Dear zoo* (Rod Campbell) — adjectives to describe animals;
- *The bad-tempered ladybird* (Eric Carle) — different animals and descriptions of them, telling the time.

Of course, you may have decided that you have had enough of animals and want to move to a different theme. What is sure is that you will find a story to link into your chosen theme and that you will be able to build on the foreign language skills developed in the activities surrounding the story of *Monsieur Beauregard*.

One final thing . . . you can be sure that next time you ask '*Are you sitting comfortably?*' and go on to say . . .

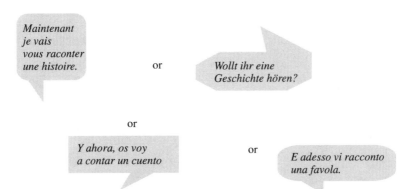

. . . your pupils will be glad that you have been converted to storytelling as part of your foreign language programme.

References

Useful sources

Modern languages in the primary school (SOED/SCOPE, 1993)
3 videos and viewing guide

Modern languages in the primary school (SOED/SCOPE/SITC, 1994)
3 CDi and viewing guide

Modern languages in the primary school (SOED/SCET, 1993)
The national training programmes in French, German, Italian, Spanish

CDi Staff development French (SOED/SITC)
CDi package to be published early 1996

Resources

Chantez OK (Mary Glasgow Publications, 1993)
Cassette of songs

Ideas practicas para la clase de español (Mary Glasgow Publications, 1991)
Book of visual repromasters

Idee pratiche per lezioni d'italiano (Mary Glasgow Publications, 1991)
Book of visual repromasters

Ideés pratiques pour la classe de français (Mary Glasgow Publications, 1991)
Book of visual repromasters

Praktische Ideen für den Deutschunterricht (Mary Glasgow Publications, 1991)
Book of visual repromasters

Miniflashcard language games
Miniflashcard Games, PO Box 1526, London W17 1ND.

Delbende J-C and V Heuze, *Le francais en chantant* (Didier/European Schoolbooks, 1992), cassette of songs + activities book and teacher's guide

Fisher J, *Lesekiste* (Mary Glasgow Publications, 1986)
Readers and teacher's guide